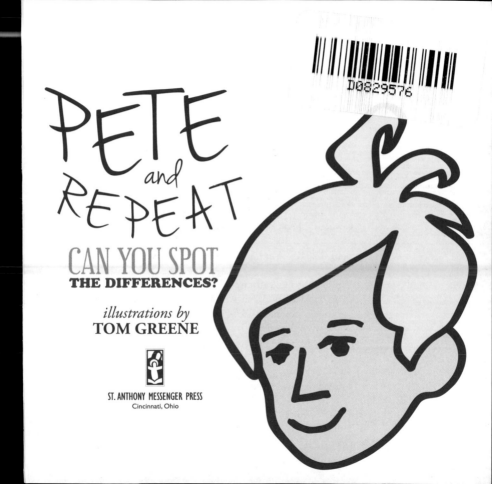

PETE and REPEAT

CAN YOU SPOT THE DIFFERENCES?

illustrations by
TOM GREENE

ST. ANTHONY MESSENGER PRESS
Cincinnati, Ohio

Cover and book design by Mark Sullivan

Published by St. Anthony Messenger Press
28 W. Liberty St.
Cincinnati, OH 45202
www.AmericanCatholic.org
www.SAMPBooks.org

Printed in the United States of America.

Printed on acid-free paper.

12 13 14 15 16   5 4 3 2 1

Introduction

These Scenes May Seem Alike to You...

In the late 1800s few could imagine that *St. Anthony Messenger* magazine would grow to become a national publication and would last for so long! I suppose the same might be said for a lively feature that first appeared in January 1959, "Pete and Repeat."

Pete was a collaborative effort from the beginning. The editors were inspired then in concept and rhyme by a German Franciscan magazine whose title is lost from memory. The art originally came from that magazine. Editor Victor Drees, O.F.M., his assistant, Marie Frohmiller, and young assistant editor Mary Lynne Phillips came up with Pete's English-language rhyme scheme—a new verse for each month followed by a standard, rhyming challenge. In the early 1970s, illustrator Tom Greene was recruited and has been illustrating Pete ever since. Hundreds of thousands of subscribers over all these years have opened their magazine and turned first to "Pete and Repeat."

The process of creating Pete starts with the rhyme; the illustration follows. Each month, Tom receives a verse and then, a few weeks later, drops by *St. Anthony Messenger*'s Cincinnati editorial offices, in the Over-the-Rhine neighborhood, with a new panel. The staff here does the rest, making a copy of the image and then (with knife and pen in the early years) introducing subtle changes they challenge readers to identify. (Now, of course, it's scanned and modified digitally.)

The rhyme has its own history: Eventually Mary Lynne Rapien (now married) was assigned to create the rhymes on her own. Sometimes her growing family came up with verses at the dinner table! In the 1970s the rhymes, still concocted by Rapien, came under the direction of then–managing editor Barbara Beckwith and, many years later, landed with managing editor Susan Hines-Brigger, whose rhymes appear in this book. Susan says she spends as much time creating that rhyme each month as she does with many of her editing tasks!

Pete changed with the times. He was a variety of goofy adults in the beginning; eventually he became a young lad and stayed that way. Sis was introduced and, in recent years, Scruffy the dog. Pete went digital along with everyone else in the 1990s, and then went full-color when color became affordable. (We quickly were chastised by a few of our color-blind readers to be sure the changes would show up for them, too.)

Ours wasn't the first use of the Pete and Repeat tagline—there was a 1931 film directed by the famed silent film star Fatty Arbuckle (he discovered Charlie Chaplain), the incessantly recited joke about Pete and Repeat falling off the boat (which now shows up even on YouTube), a repetitive parrot toy, a few drinking bars, and a rock band. But Pete has probably had his longest life in *St. Anthony Messenger*. We hope you'll enjoy this rich serving of our favorite feature!

—John Feister, editor-in-chief, *St. Anthony Messenger*

New Year's Day
Pete and Sis have found a way
To celebrate on New Year's Day.
They'll gather family, friends, and all
To play a game of flag football.

These scenes may seem alike to you,
But there are changes in the two.
So look and see if you can name
Eight ways in which they're not the same.

1

Winter Playtime

Pete and Sis are set to play
Outside on this wintry day.
With lots of snow upon the ground,
They'll build a snowman big and round.

These scenes may seem alike to you,
But there are changes in the two.
So look and see if you can name
Eight ways in which they're not the same.

Warm Fireside

3

Pete and Scruffy leap and bound
Through the snow upon the ground.
When they're done they'll go inside
To warm up by the fireside.

These scenes may seem alike to you,
But there are changes in the two.
So look and see if you can name
Eight ways in which they're not the same.

Carriage Ride
Pete and Sis see friends outside
On a horse-drawn carriage ride.
They bundle up and join the fun
As through the snow the horses run.

These scenes may seem alike to you,
But there are changes in the two.
So look and see if you can name
Eight ways in which they're not the same.

4

Super Bowl
Pete and friends are gathered near
The TV so they all can cheer.
They'll whoop and cheer with great delight
Because the Super Bowl's tonight.

These scenes may seem alike to you,
But there are changes in the two.
So look and see if you can name
Eight ways in which they're not the same.

5

Valentine's Day
With Valentine's around the bend,
Pete and Sis prepare to send
A little bit of love and cheer
In notes to all whom they hold dear.

These scenes may seem alike to you,
But there are changes in the two.
So look and see if you can name
Eight ways in which they're not the same.

6

Helping a Neighbor

Pete decided he will go
Outside to help shovel snow.
He'll help the neighbors clear the way
On this cold and snowy day.

These scenes may seem alike to you,
But there are changes in the two.
So look and see if you can name
Eight ways in which they're not the same.

A Tiny Friend
Pete's excited he has found
A caterpillar on the ground.
One day it will reach the sky
When it becomes a butterfly.

These scenes may seem alike to you,
But there are changes in the two.
So look and see if you can name
Eight ways in which they're not the same.

8

Signs of Spring
While outside walking Pete has found
Flowers poking through the ground.
With signs that spring is on its way,
Pete soaks up this glorious day.

These scenes may seem alike to you,
But there are changes in the two.
So look and see if you can name
Eight ways in which they're not the same.

Outdoor Fun

Now that spring is on its way,
Pete is going out to play.
He'll run around with all his friends
Until the day comes to an end.

These scenes may seem alike to you,
But there are changes in the two.
So look and see if you can name
Eight ways in which they're not the same.

10

Gathering Blooms
Now that spring has come to town
Flowers pop up from the ground.
So Pete is going to spend the day
Gathering up a big bouquet.

These scenes may seem alike to you,
But there are changes in the two.
So look and see if you can name
Eight ways in which they're not the same.

11

A Visit to the Garden Store

Pete and Sis are on their way
To the garden store today.
They'll spend time searching long and hard
For flowers to plant in their yard.

These scenes may seem alike to you,
But there are changes in the two.
So look and see if you can name
Eight ways in which they're not the same.

12

Rainy Day

Because the rain won't go away,
Pete is stuck inside today.
He'll find a book he hasn't read,
And curl up tight upon his bed.

These scenes may seem alike to you,
But there are changes in the two.
So look and see if you can name
Eight ways in which they're not the same.

13

Baseball Season

Pete has been waiting ever since fall
To hear the wonderful words, "Play ball."
With ticket in hand he'll search for his seat,
Then cheer on his team while having a treat.

These scenes may seem alike to you,
But there are changes in the two.
So look and see if you can name
Eight ways in which they're not the same.

14

Easter Time

15

Pete and Sis have come inside
To make sure all the eggs are dyed.
They'll fix the baskets up with care,
With eggs and lots of treats to share.

These scenes may seem alike to you,
But there are changes in the two.
So look and see if you can name
Eight ways in which they're not the same.

Riding a Bike

Now that spring is finally here,
Pete and Sis let out a cheer.
They'll get to do the things they like,
Like go outside and ride a bike.

These scenes may seem alike to you,
But there are changes in the two.
So look and see if you can name
Eight ways in which they're not the same.

16

Something for Mom
Pete is looking all around
At flowers bursting through the ground.
With Mother's Day not far away
He'll pick some for his mom today.

17

These scenes may seem alike to you,
But there are changes in the two.
So look and see if you can name
Eight ways in which they're not the same.

Spring Cleaning
Pete is bustling all about,
Trying to help his mother out.
He cleaned his room and swept the floor
And now he's set to clean some more.

These scenes may seem alike to you,
But there are changes in the two.
So look and see if you can name
Eight ways in which they're not the same.

18

Mother's Day
To honor Mom on Mother's Day,
Pete and Sis will spend the day
Cooking up a fancy meal
To let her know just how they feel.

These scenes may seem alike to you,
But there are changes in the two.
So look and see if you can name
Eight ways in which they're not the same.

19

Big Brother

As a way to show he cares,
Pete bought Sis a teddy bear.
No matter what, they'll always be
Part of one big family.

These scenes may seem alike to you,
But there are changes in the two.
So look and see if you can name
Eight ways in which they're not the same.

20

Memorial Day

21

Pete and friends have found a way
To celebrate Memorial Day.
They head off with some flags in hand
To honor those who served our land.

These scenes may seem alike to you,
But there are changes in the two.
So look and see if you can name
Eight ways in which they're not the same.

School's Out
Now that school is finally done,
Pete is soaking up the sun.
He'll spend his days out by the pool
Having fun while staying cool.

These scenes may seem alike to you,
But there are changes in the two.
So look and see if you can name
Eight ways in which they're not the same.

Lazy Summer Day
Pete is lying on the ground
Soaking up the summer sounds.
He's looking up into the sky,
And watching all the clouds drift by.

These scenes may seem alike to you,
But there are changes in the two.
So look and see if you can name
Eight ways in which they're not the same.

A Visit to the Shore

Pete is standing on the shore,
Listening to the ocean's roar.
While staring out at sea from land,
He recognizes God's great hand.

These scenes may seem alike to you,
But there are changes in the two.
So look and see if you can name
Eight ways in which they're not the same.

24

Neighborhood Cookout

Pete's friends will all gather soon,
On this sunny day in June.
Pete will fire up the grill
Till everyone has had their fill.

These scenes may seem alike to you,
But there are changes in the two.
So look and see if you can name
Eight ways in which they're not the same.

25

Hard at Work

Pete is outside working hard,
Helping mow the neighbor's yard.
The money earned will help him buy
A brand-new bike that caught his eye.

These scenes may seem alike to you,
But there are changes in the two.
So look and see if you can name
Eight ways in which they're not the same.

26

Fourth of July
On this Independence Day
Pete and Sis will shout, "Hurray!"
With their friends they'll watch the sky
As fireworks begin to fly.

These scenes may seem alike to you,
But there are changes in the two.
So look and see if you can name
Eight ways in which they're not the same.

27

A Special Treat
Pete and Sis walk down the street
To go and buy an ice cream treat.
They think that it's the perfect way
To try to beat the heat today.

These scenes may seem alike to you,
But there are changes in the two.
So look and see if you can name
Eight ways in which they're not the same.

28

Flying Kites

Pete and Sis go out to play
On this clear and sunny day.
They fly their homemade kites with ease
On the steady summer breeze.

These scenes may seem alike to you,
But there are changes in the two.
So look and see if you can name
Eight ways in which they're not the same.

29

Helping Out

Pete is going to volunteer
For a cause that he holds dear.
He'll team up with the local vet
To help people adopt a pet.

These scenes may seem alike to you,
But there are changes in the two.
So look and see if you can name
Eight ways in which they're not the same.

30

A Trip to the Fair

Pete and Sis are at the fair
Trying to win a big stuffed bear.
They'll play some games and go on rides,
Like racing down the giant slides.

These scenes may seem alike to you,
But there are changes in the two.
So look and see if you can name
Eight ways in which they're not the same.

31

Grandma's House

32

Pete and Sis are on their way
To visit with Grandma today.
They're bringing treats that they can share
To let her know how much they care.

These scenes may seem alike to you,
But there are changes in the two.
So look and see if you can name
Eight ways in which they're not the same.

Back-to-School Shopping

Pete and Sis are on their way
To shop for school supplies today.
Before too long they'll be in school
Instead of sitting by the pool.

These scenes may seem alike to you,
But there are changes in the two.
So look and see if you can name
Eight ways in which they're not the same.

33

A Lazy Summer Day

Pete enjoys the gentle breeze
Blowing through the backyard trees.
A hammock's where he'll spend the day,
As summer days just slip away.

These scenes may seem alike to you,
But there are changes in the two.
So look and see if you can name
Eight ways in which they're not the same.

34

Last Days of Summer
As summertime draws to an end
Pete and Sis will try to spend
The days before they head to school
Just having fun and keeping cool.

These scenes may seem alike to you,
But there are changes in the two.
So look and see if you can name
Eight ways in which they're not the same.

35

First Day of School

36

All summer long Pete's had his fun,
But now those laid-back days are done.
Pete and his friends will make their way
To school because it starts today.

These scenes may seem alike to you,
But there are changes in the two.
So look and see if you can name
Eight ways in which they're not the same.

Football Fun
Since the school year has begun,
Pete and Sis are having fun.
On Friday nights they yell and scream
And cheer on their school's football team.

These scenes may seem alike to you,
But there are changes in the two.
So look and see if you can name
Eight ways in which they're not the same.

37

Helping Animals

Pete and Sis are working hard
To welcome critters to their yard.
They'll hang feeders in the trees,
For all the many birds to see.

These scenes may seem alike to you,
But there are changes in the two.
So look and see if you can name
Eight ways in which they're not the same.

38

Harvest Time

Pete and Sis are working hard
Gathering bounty from the yard.
The vegetables they grew from seed
Will now be sent to those in need.

These scenes may seem alike to you,
But there are changes in the two.
So look and see if you can name
Eight ways in which they're not the same.

39

Fresh Air
Instead of lying 'round all day,
Pete has gone outside to play.
Taking time to jump and run
Is sure to lead to lots of fun.

These scenes may seem alike to you,
But there are changes in the two.
So look and see if you can name
Eight ways in which they're not the same.

40

Volunteering

Pete and Sis will take a stand
And help out those who need a hand.
As they have for many years,
They'll do good work as volunteers.

These scenes may seem alike to you,
But there are changes in the two.
So look and see if you can name
Eight ways in which they're not the same.

41

Pumpkin Patch

Pete and Sis will make their way
To the pumpkin patch today.
They'll carefully look upon the ground
Until the perfect pumpkin's found.

These scenes may seem alike to you,
But there are changes in the two.
So look and see if you can name
Eight ways in which they're not the same.

42

Halloween

Pete and Sis and all their friends
Will walk the street from end to end.
They'll stop at every house they know,
And gather candy as they go.

These scenes may seem alike to you,
But there are changes in the two.
So look and see if you can name
Eight ways in which they're not the same.

43

Election Day
With school elections drawing near
Pete speaks to issues he holds dear.
Both better food and more green space
Are major issues in this race.

These scenes may seem alike to you,
But there are changes in the two.
So look and see if you can name
Eight ways in which they're not the same.

44

Veterans Day

Pete and Sis have gathered 'round
To read the stories they have found
Of Grandpa's years spent in the war
And battles fought on distant shores.

These scenes may seem alike to you,
But there are changes in the two.
So look and see if you can name
Eight ways in which they're not the same

45

Thanksgiving Day

Pete has found a special way
To celebrate Thanksgiving Day.
He'll offer up a heartfelt prayer
For friends and family gathered there.

These scenes may seem alike to you,
But there are changes in the two.
So look and see if you can name
Eight ways in which they're not the same.

46

Family Memories
Pete and family gather 'round
A book of photos they have found.
As they look, they'll reminisce
About fun times and those they miss.

These scenes may seem alike to you,
But there are changes in the two.
So look and see if you can name
Eight ways in which they're not the same.

47

Decorating the House

On this cold and wintry night,
Pete and family hang their lights.
They'll go inside and grab a cup
Of cocoa to help warm them up.

These scenes may seem alike to you,
But there are changes in the two.
So look and see if you can name
Eight ways in which they're not the same.

48

The Giving Tree
In hopes of lifting spirits high,
Pete and Sis have gone to buy
Presents for the giving tree
To spread a little Christmas glee.

These scenes may seem alike to you,
But there are changes in the two.
So look and see if you can name
Eight ways in which they're not the same.

Seeing the Sights

Pete and Sis will go tonight
With Mom and Dad to look at lights.
Afterward they'll drive to see
If they can find a Christmas tree.

These scenes may seem alike to you,
But there are changes in the two.
So look and see if you can name
Eight ways in which they're not the same.

50

Trimming the Tree

Pete and Sis adorn the tree
With sparkling lights for all to see.
They'll place the manger down below
Beneath the branches all aglow.

These scenes may seem alike to you,
But there are changes in the two.
So look and see if you can name
Eight ways in which they're not the same.

51

Christmas Day

Mom and Dad watch Pete and Sis
Unwrap all their Christmas gifts.
When they're done, they'll take a ride
To see the Christmas lights outside.

These scenes may seem alike to you,
But there are changes in the two.
So look and see if you can name
Eight ways in which they're not the same.

Answer Key

1: New Year's Day
1. The door casing is visible.
2. Sis has unbuttoned her sweater.
3. Sis has moved her right foot.
4. The player chasing Pete has hair outside his collar.
5. Pete's friend no longer has cuffed pants.
6. The lacing on Pete's football isn't visible.
7. Pete's left wrist can be seen.
8. Pete's hair is off his forehead a bit more.

2: Winter Playtime
1. The snowman has his right arm.
2. The snowman's right eye is lower.
3. The snowman's left arm is higher.
4. Sis's hat has fur trim.
5. Sis has a vest over her sweater.
6. Scruffy makes an appearance.
7. Pete's scarf has no fringe.
8. The snow is deeper near Pete's leg.

3: Warm Fireside
1. Drapes have more folds.
2. It's dark outside.
3. Drapes hang down near Pete's ear.
4. The fire has a smaller flame.
5. The hearth has one longer brick.
6. The room has a baseboard.
7. Part of Pete's shirt has changed color.
8. Scruffy went back out in the snow.

4: Carriage Ride
1. Sis's headband is a different color.
2. A snowflake near Sis's head has melted.
3. Snow is gone from the window pane above Pete's head.
4. The curtain covers the woodwork.

5. The red hood one friend wears covers more of her head.
6. The other friend now holds both reins.
7. Pete has parted his hair.
8. Scruffy is peeking out the window, too.

5: Super Bowl
1. A lamp has appeared in the corner.
2. The portrait has been hung lower on wall.
3. More remodeling: The room has a chair rail.
4. Penalty! An extra player is on the field.
5. Dark trim now edges the floor.
6. One piece of popcorn has been eaten.
7. Pete's beverage is on the table.
8. Pete's buddy is looking down.

6: Valentine's Day
1. There's a reflection in the window.
2. Pete's shirt has become two colors.
3. The right curtain has one fewer fold.
4. Sis is wearing a ring.
5. Sis has lace on her collar.
6. The blank paper near Sis has been moved.
7. The small heart on another paper has been moved.
8. Pete has drawn a large heart on his paper.

7: Helping a Neighbor
1. The shovel has a blue stripe.
2. It's getting dark.
3. Pete's hand is lower on the shovel.
4. Scruffy has appeared.
5. A line is missing from the sidewalk.
6. The horizon is higher.
7. The door has a window.
8. Pete can see his breath.

8: A Tiny Friend
1. One of the butterfly's antennae has changed.
2. A squirrel is in the tree.
3. Pete's shirt collar is different.
4. Pete's sock is visible.
5. All of Pete's right fingers are curved down.
6. One less bubble connects Pete to butterfly image.
7. Another blade of grass has popped up.
8. The most distant hill has disappeared.

9: Signs of Spring
1. A twig has broken off the tree.
2. Another cloud has appeared on the horizon.
3. The tree now has a knothole.
4. A kite is flying in the distance.
5. The bird has moved away from Pete.
6. On fence, two stones at top are now one.
7. There's a crease in Pete's left shirtsleeve.
8. The smallest yellow flower has a new leaf.

10: Outdoor Fun
1. Part of the kite is white.
2. A bird is near the kite.
3. The kite's tail is shorter.
4. The left cloud is lower.
5. The hole in the cloud moved.
6. The handle on the reel is up.
7. The tree has an extra branch.
8. The cloud has another hole.

11: Gathering Blooms
1. The red house is now two stories.
2. The home's front door is visible.
3. Pete has pushed his hair back from his eye.
4. Pete's left sleeve has another crease at the elbow.
5. One leaf is missing from center of bouquet.
6. A new leaf is added to bouquet in back.
7. The heel of Pete's right shoe can be seen.
8. Two stones in wall are now one.

12: A Visit to the Garden Store
1. The border of the raised bed has an extra board.
2. There's a new sapling.
3. A bird has flown near the trees.
4. The greenhouse is missing a support bar.
5. Pete's waistband has disappeared.
6. A plank is visible in the picnic table.
7. The flower Pete has picked up is taller.
8. The flower in front has lost a leaf.

13: Rainy Day
1. The light is turned on.
2. Both curtain panels can be seen.
3. A second book is on Pete's bed.
4. The binding on Pete's blanket is visible.
5. Pete's hair is pushed back.
6. Pete's pants have a pocket.
7. Pete also has cuffed pants.
8. The title of Pete's book is on its spine.

14: Baseball Season
1. A bird is flying near the grandstand.
2. There's a loudspeaker on the grandstand.
3. A shingle on the grandstand is missing.
4. The home team has two runs on the scoreboard.
5. Pete's hot dog has mustard on it.
6. Pete is wearing a vest.
7. The sleeve of Pete's shirt is yellow.
8. The redhead in the last row is not there.

15: Easter Time
1. Sis has moved her right arm.
2. Sis's jumper has a round neckline.
3. The table is shorter at Sis's end.
4. One piece of candy has moved closer to the others.
5. The colors on candy-bar wrapper are reversed.
6. One of Pete's eggs is marked with a cross.
7. Pete's basket has a piece of candy in it.
8. Pete's shirt has a wrinkle at his right arm.

16: Riding a Bike
1. Sis sees a butterfly near her arm.
2. One branch is missing near top of tree.
3. A large branch above Pete is lower.
4. Pete has tucked in his shirt.
5. A fallen flower petal has blown away.
6. One flower has grown much taller than the others.
7. Sis is wearing a kneepad.
8. The bicycle now has a headlight.

17: Something for Mom
1. The tree's leaves have moved on the left.
2. An orange butterfly has appeared.
3. There's a knothole in the fence.
4. One of the yellow flowers has lost a petal.
5. The red flower on the left is taller.
6. The edge of a fence board has disappeared.
7. Pete's collar is different.
8. A pocket on Pete's pants is visible.

18: Spring Cleaning
1. A curtain fold on the left is gone.
2. The broom handle is longer.
3. There's a bird outside the window.
4. Pete has a cuff on his left sleeve.
5. The cleaning solution has moved.
6. The pail is emptied of water.
7. Mom's wedding ring is visible.
8. Her collar is white.

19: Mother's Day
1. Mom's glasses are gone.
2. Her collar has become lavender.
3. Sis is wearing a cross.
4. Pete has added a vest.
5. Mom's fork has disappeared.
6. Her orange juice is now milk.
7. There's another muffin.
8. The vase has moved.

20: Big Brother
1. The mirror has a streak on it.
2. Pete brushed his hair out of his eye.
3. Pete's shirt pocket is on the opposite side.
4. The window in the door is shorter.
5. Sis's blouse can be seen near her elbow.
6. The teddy bear has a rounded belly.
7. The bear has a bow around his neck.
8. Teddy's eye is closed.

21: Memorial Day
1. Sis's cuff is now part of her sleeve.
2. Sis's headband has disappeared.
3. A serviceman in the back is missing.
4. Another has put on his medals.
5. Pete has a button on his shirt.
6. Pete wears a wristwatch on his left arm.
7. Pete's friend has an extra fold in his shirt.
8. His pants have changed color.

22: School's Out
1. Slim tree trunk is gone.
2. A path now leads to the house.
3. One more ripple has been created.
4. Pete's waistband is a different color.
5. Pete's swim trunks have one fewer spot.
6. Pete has turned the beach ball.
7. The hill behind Pete is higher.
8. A bird flies by.

23: Lazy Summer Day
1. The tree has a new opening through the leaves.
2. The cloud formation has shifted.
3. Someone's flying a kite near the horizon.
4. Pete's shorts now have one stripe.
5. Scruffy is looking up.
6. Pete has put on his sunglasses.
7. One flower's leaf has gotten longer.
8. A bee buzzes near the flowers.

24: A Visit to the Shore
1. The tree trunk has lost a bud scale scar.
2. The sun is higher in the sky.
3. One bird has flown away from the scene.
4. More sky is visible within the cloud formation.
5. A skier has appeared on the water.
6. Scruffy has come to the shore.
7. The design on the right leg of Pete's swim trunks has changed.
8. Pete has put on his sunglasses.

25: Neighborhood Cookout
1. Tree's leaves allow in less sunlight.
2. Pete is now wearing one oven mitt.
3. Part of grilling rack is missing.
4. A hot dog has appeared on the rack.
5. Sis has a white collar on her dress.
6. She's holding a plate, ready for the food.
7. Boy watching from the back wears a cap.
8. The rock wall below him has changed.

26: Hard at Work
1. Another window shutter is visible.
2. Scruffy has come out on the walkway.
3. Pete is now looking down.
4. His shirt collar has turned white.
5. The mower handle is black.
6. A butterfly has appeared on the right.
7. The neighbor's child has short sleeves.
8. He's also changed into shorts.

27: Fourth of July
1. Another burst of fireworks has lit up the sky.
2. A second cluster of fireworks is higher.
3. Scruffy has leaped into Pete's arms.
4. Branches in the distant trees are different.
5. Sis's sundress isn't scooped in back.
6. Pete's friend waves back to him.
7. The friend's collar has changed.
8. The friend's nose is now visible.

28: A Special Treat
1. Tree trunk nearest ice cream stand has moved.
2. A tree has appeared behind building.
3. Last letter of ICE is reversed.
4. Snowflake has been added to building décor.
5. Giant cone is dripping ice cream from bottom.
6. Sis is pointing to ice cream stand.
7. Sis's left ear is now visible.
8. Top stripe is missing from Pete's sleeve.

29: Flying Kites
1. Scruffy has entered the scene on the left.
2. Pete is now wearing a watch.
3. The sun has moved.
4. A bird has flown near the sun.
5. The girl's skirt has changed into shorts.
6. There's a new break in the trees behind her.
7. Part of the kite's string is now behind the clouds.
8. The last pennant on its tail has changed color.

30: Helping Out
1. The E of VET on the door is flipped.
2. The vet's diploma has another line of type.
3. His coat has turned blue.
4. The coat has gained a pocket.
5. Pete's collar is visible.
6. The girl now has a hair barrette.
7. The cat has lost a stripe.
8. The cat's tail has moved.

31: A Trip to the Fair
1. The armadillo's tail is curled upward.
2. The colored ball has spun so the colored quarters have shifted.
3. Sis's dress has another gather in skirt.
4. The counter ledge now has a sill.
5. The toy plane has a stripe.
6. Pete has changed to long pants.
7. Pete's shirt is missing one red spot.
8. Pete holds a second hoop in his left hand.

32: Grandma's House
1. A brick is missing to the left of the door.
2. A bush has grown to the door's left.
3. A full-grown tree appears on the right.
4. There's a handrail next to Grandma's hand.
5. A sidewalk now runs out from the steps.
6. Grandma's apron has a pocket.
7. Sis's sleeve has a ruffle.
8. Pete's shirt has lost one of its squares.

33: Back-to-School Shopping
1. Scruffy has jumped into the pool!
2. The imaginary Sis is wearing sunglasses.
3. The pool has one fewer ripples.
4. Pete's shirt has a crew neck.
5. Sis is missing her button.
6. One car has changed colors.
7. A parking stripe is visible between cars.
8. The car nearest to Sis has lost its tailpipe.

34: A Lazy Summer Day
1. The horizon behind Pete is higher.
2. There is another bird.
3. Pete is now wearing sunglasses.
4. His top has changed to a V-neck.
5. There is a stripe down his shorts.
6. A book is beside him on the hammock.
7. The table has gone from square to round.
8. There's another ice cube in his lemonade.

35: Last Days of Summer
1. A bird flies by in the distance.
2. Scruffy tries to join the picnic.
3. Hill behind Sis is lower.
4. An ear of corn is missing.
5. Sis has some lemonade.
6. One red check is gone from tablecloth.
7. Thermos has dark stripe at bottom.
8. Spigot on thermos is not visible.

36: First Day of School
1. A button is missing on Pete's schoolbag.
2. There's an extra cloud puff.
3. A second sky hole has opened in the clouds.
4. A person has appeared in the left window.
5. Another person is visible in a middle window.
6. The girl has a V-neck top.
7. Her skirt has a ruffle.
8. The boy's lunchbox is smaller.

37: Football Fun
1. The stadium has an additional floodlight.
2. A fan seated at top left has left her seat.
3. The sky is dark.
4. A fan is now seated in top row at right.
5. Sis's left sleeve is shorter.
6. Sis's skirt has an emblem on it.
7. Pete's megaphone now has a dark stripe.
8. Pete's shirt has a dark elbow patch.

38: Helping Animals
1. A new bird is flying between the branches.
2. The red bird now has a yellow chest.
3. The bushes have grown behind Pete.
4. There's a knothole on the tree.
5. The feeder has more food on the right.
6. Pete's feeder has an opening and a perch.
7. Scruffy has joined the action.
8. Sis's feeder now sports a hook.

39: Harvest Time
1. The most distant skyline is lower.
2. One bird has flown south.
3. Pete is warmer in a turtleneck.
4. One apple is missing from Pete's basket.
5. There's an additional ridge on the horizon.
6. Sis is warmer with long sleeves.
7. An apple has rolled into the vegetable cart.
8. Another potato has been added to the harvest.

40: Fresh Air
1. The bushes behind Pete are higher.
2. Pete's right sleeve has a fold at the elbow.
3. A football is coming Pete's way.
4. One bird is nearer the roof of the building.
5. An opening in the tree's foliage is larger.
6. One tree trunk is no longer visible.
7. The sidewalk from the building is gone.
8. Sis's left leg has moved.

41: Volunteering
1. A bird is flying behind Pete.
2. His shirt has a white stripe.
3. He is now wearing a watch.
4. The tree is taller.
5. The sun is higher.
6. The white collar on the red-shirted boy has turned red.
7. He is holding a new piece of trash.
8. Sis is wearing a ring.

42: Pumpkin Patch
1. The barn now has a silo.
2. A man on a tractor is leaving the barn.
3. The corn shock toward the back is taller.
4. Pete's pants are a darker color.
5. The pumpkin in front has rolled toward Pete.
6. Sis's pumpkin has become a jack-o'-lantern.
7. Sis has pulled up her sock.
8. One more pumpkin has appeared near Sis.

43: Halloween
1. Two bricks are now one.
2. The light fixture has a new decoration.
3. Pete has lifted his mask.
4. Pete is wearing black rather than white.
5. The door handle is visible.
6. Someone took a piece of Pete's candy!
7. The pirate's vest colors are reversed.
8. The skull on the pirate's hat wears an eye patch.

44: Election Day
1. The flag has an extra stripe.
2. The flag is longer on the right.
3. Pete's microphone has moved to the other side.
4. Pete now sports a pocket handkerchief.
5. He's wearing a tie clasp.
6. The front of the podium has changed.
7. The listener on the left is now totally bald.
8. The redhead has lost her cowlick.

45: Veterans Day
1. The hair on Pete's forehead is fuller.
2. Sis is wearing a white shirt under her sweater.
3. Sis's headband is gone.
4. Book has a picture.
5. Time has changed on the clock.
6. Grandpa has a turtleneck under his shirt.
7. Grandpa's shirt has an extra button.
8. There's a line missing from a brick under Grandpa's foot.

46: Thanksgiving Day
1. The spindle of Pete's chair is visible.
2. Pete has removed his tie.
3. Pete has a plate.
4. Sis pushed her hair behind her ear.
5. Sis's right arm can be seen.
6. The youngest guest's knife and spoon are reversed.
7. This guest's hair has changed color.
8. Mom's dress is also a different hue.

47: Family Memories
1. The back of the couch is higher.
2. Mom's collar has shrunk.
3. She's wearing a butterfly pin.
4. Pete's hair is not covering his eye.
5. One of the photos is crooked.
6. The binding of the album is visible.
7. Sis is wearing a bracelet.
8. She now has a ruffle on her sleeve.

48: Decorating the House
1. The left curtain is less full.
2. Twilight has become night.
3. Sis has a yellow collar.
4. Steam is rising from Sis's mug.
5. The handle of her mug shows.
6. A yellow bulb has become green.
7. A new yellow Christmas light has sprung up.
8. Pete's button is missing from his coat.

49: The Giving Tree
1. Light switch is visible on the left.
2. Ribbon streamer on the left is shorter.
3. Pete's left arm shows.
4. Scruffy has appeared next to Pete's leg.
5. Night has fallen.
6. A red ornament near the top of the tree is gone.
7. A picture is now on the wall.
8. Another package wrapped in green has appeared.

50: Seeing the Sights
1. One more light shines on strand above trees.
2. Night has fallen.
3. On tree nearest Sis, a branch is no longer visible in second tier from top.
4. Sis is trying to poke Pete with her elbow.
5. The belt on Pete's coat is gone.
6. Pete has put on earmuffs.
7. Dad has grown a beard.
8. Mom has misplaced her large purse.

51: Trimming the Tree
1. Sis's shoulder can be seen.
2. Sis has moved one green Christmas bulb.
3. Pete now has a white-collared shirt under his sweater.
4. Pete has removed one yellow Christmas bulb.
5. Red garland can be seen between Pete's knees.
6. The Christmas tree skirt is a darker hue.
7. St. Joseph holds a staff.
8. Scruffy has come to visit the manger scene.

52: Christmas Day
1. The curtain is smaller.
2. Night has fallen.
3. A floorboard is gone.
4. Pete swept his hair back off his forehead.
5. The Christmas tree has an extra branch.
6. The tree is missing an ornament.
7. The ribbon in Sis's hand is longer.
8. A stripe is gone from Pete's present.